Silkworm's Pansori

(American Sijo)

David Seung

The Song Cave

The Song Cave
www.the-song-cave.com

Design and layout by Janet Evans-Scanlon

ISBN: 979-8-9912988-1-0
Library of Congress Cataloguing-in-Publication Data has been applied for.

FIRST PRINTING

Contents

繭

絲

Preface

The sijo is Korea's most prominent and enduring traditional poetic form. My ambition to advance the sijo within the English literary canon is not for the sake of the form itself, but for the benefit of English literature, which at the time of this book's conception is notably deficient in regards to the sijo and its unique offerings, affordances, distillations and sensibilities.

Sijo are inherently accessible. They are clear and straightforward with their language and syntax, while remaining emotionally nuanced and playfully (albeit ruefully) layered. Their complexity comes from complication of meaning and feeling. It is a form of subtleties, and was, perhaps for that reason, the primary poetic medium of kisaeng in an older Korea, although maybe the causality of that relationship is the other way around. Kisaeng were in an interesting liminal social position, able to exist among higher social classes and navigate the tight hegemony of Choson-dynasty society as female artist-entertainers/hostesses. Where the poems written by men in that era were largely trite, clichéd emulations of traditional aesthetics and Confucian values, these women were, by consequence of their exclusion from the higher social stratus, unbound in their art. Kisaeng revolutionized the form, the genre, and the canon of Korean literature through honest, free, passionate emotions, alongside their subversive and nuanced vehicles. They introduced a new degree of humor and brazenness to Korean poetry, as well as a kind of liberation from formality.

The poems in this book are English-language sijo, and before that, distinctly American sijo; they are not a survival of the tradition but an appropriation of it, and one necessarily distanced from its origin. Chef Massimo Bottura believes that "tradition ties us to a culture and place, but it must be seen from ten kilometers away." Only through a lens of liminality can we see our inheritances critically rather than nostalgically, and we need to "pry, poke, and question the authority" thereof in order to learn from the past without slipping into dogmatic emulation. While that stance was taken in the context of tortellini, the principles are universally applicable. American sijo can never be the same as Korean sijo, so they need not try to be, but can instead capitalize on the affordances of the English language and their own cultural locus, adopting what is needed or beneficial for their speciation.

The English language is flexible but unruly. Adopting a form developed for a very different mode of language is awkward. English syntax spills over the tight belt of the jueju. Stressed and unstressed syllables slosh around inside haiku and tanka. Translating the sijo form, despite its relative liberties, likewise demands some structural lenience. The sijo that exist in English tend to break the three two-part lines into three couplets, with each line within containing somewhere between six and nine syllables. Linda Sue Park, author of *Tap Dancing on the Roof*, prefers to count stressed syllables, placing three or four in each line segment (with varying line structures). This approach is in line with the original rhythm and voice of traditional sijo, which, when sung and performed in a pansori context, would feature long sustains on key words while bouncing relatively quickly over others. Despite Korean not being a stress-timed language, the performance of sijo still necessarily created an inequality of syllabic emphasis. I have, for the most part, attempted to preserve some of the sijo's innate musicality, balance, and rhythm through syllabic curation, often using the six-to-nine syllable range for individual lines as a constraint. My priority in translating the form is preserving the three-part structure of introduction, development, and turn, which is the heart of the sijo. I also seek to maintain the traditional sijo's characteristic nuance and gestural subtleties. Across the span of this book, I have approached my appropriation of the form with varying (structural and thematic) adherence to tradition, straying with a few prominent and recurring devices—namely, the use of enjambment, grouping, and footnotes,[1] which often become real estate for prosaic or poetic expansion. That footnote spillover, however egregious, is, in conjunction with corresponding sijo, a new kind of form unto itself—a Chicago-style sijo. The common purpose across those infractions is to provide information and semantic context necessary for fully understanding the poems, and those insertions are meant to be noticeable and noticed. They are taps on the shoulder to correct posture—reminders that one's experience and understanding of a poem are dependent on a knowledge of what exists beyond it. They signal the poems' own reliance on that exegesis and are, in that regard, admissions of failure.

---

1 Someone I tried to fully love espoused Gödel's incompleteness theorems as proof of the potential for the existence of a god, as the necessary failures and limitations of axiomatic theories suggest or at least afford the extra-mathematical existence of some unknowable absolute. Something like, "the notion of imperfection suggests that perfection exists." Given the inherent incompleteness of axiomatic systems, it follows that our mathematics are something constructed rather than discovered—reins we weave in an attempt to tame and understand something externally extant in the natural world. Ergo, truth exists where language fails us. Ergo, we fail truthfully. Ergo what she called love was proof that I might find it elsewhere. Etc. Etc. I know I can't do her justice.

冬至 섯달 기나긴 밤을 한 허리를 잘라 내어
春風 이불 아래 서리서리 넣었다가
어론님 오신 날 밤이여든 구뷔구뷔 펴리라

—황진이 (c. 1506–c. 1560)

I wished on the moon
for something I never knew

I wished on the moon
for more than I ever knew:

A sweeter rose, a softer sky,
On April days that would not dance away

—Dorothy Parker (1893-1967)

Transubstantiation

All flesh is just digested food,
my body built from bread and juice;

my mother's silk dress
just mulberry leaves,

my kindest ambition—
sips from the cup of trembling

I only know these stories as they were given to me.

I stem from a line of rebels. Before the War portioned the peninsula, my father's father lived in a village in the North, near the Chinese border. Japan tortured him as a child because our family refused to change our name to Masuda (he would show us his right ring finger, which Japan had gripped and wrung broken). His older brother protested, furious. Japan jailed him for years. Jail and torture. Their grandfather financed the resistance and helped rebels escape. Japan took his son, my father's father's father, and tortured him for information, but he told them nothing. Japan disappeared his older brother, shot and killed his younger brother in front of him, beat him to near death, but he told them nothing. Japan left my father's father's father on the street to die. He said that he kept thinking, "I need to get back to my family" as he slugfooted through the night, punch-drunk and bloodied. A legacy of silence. My family calls me his reincarnation. I have my father's Korean name, his father's English name, his father's face. Sometimes more. Sometimes not enough. My family made sacrifices to get here, then made sacrifices here. When I was seventeen I sacrificed everything I could to try and save someone else, and when I failed and she was gone I blamed provisional impotence. To be a man, my father tells me, is to give. When the mountain gulps the train the window becomes an answer and irony suddenly vanishes. I remember that I'm always angry. Wickless. Our family's name, the one we clung to, means inheritance.

Plates of Fruit, Cut and Peeled

Persimmons on a leafless tree:
unlaid eggs in a butchered hen.

The old woman picks from the sagging
branch. The grandson skips a stone.

It rejects the pond three times, as if
it belonged on that far shore.

A First-World Disorder

Like an unburdened stomach
Taihu[2] eats its own walls—

stones catabolized into beauty
pose along the garden path.

I clot their holes with color, transfused
from the flowers behind.

---

2 太湖 (Taihu, or Lake Tai) is famous for the limestone formations it produces, which are an iconic feature of classical Chinese gardens, especially those in nearby Suzhou. While notable for their own form and aesthetic, Taihu stones are often placed alongside specific plants as part of an appreciation for the beauty of juxtaposition, the harmony created by difference. The profundity of a stone's form comes from its context.

New American Hatreds

replaced his missing teeth.
He can't tell me how they hurt him—

eyes like a market fish—but he felt
"so ugly." To save us from his hate

he married a white woman,
circumcised our tongues.

A Tourist in My Family's House

A Different First Language

Tea leaves learn their taste from water—
a mindful sip hears three voices:

silver needle, Mt. Hood snowmelt,
the still lip of a glazed cup.

These leaves steeped in foreign waters
would speak with an accent.

"You can't even pronounce your own names"

"내 이름은 기성입니다"
승기성, like sung key-song

each sound a step down wet stairs
with the old man's half-weight in hand—

a lie I practiced in the shower
pretending my soaked hair was black

I watched him die over FaceTime

The last thing he saw was my absence.
When I called out, his eyes unsheathed

; seeing it was just a voice
he dropped his head. Went to sleep.

The last time I was there we just
sat. Ate. Few words in common.

A Selfish Elegy:
I was required to grieve differently

It was like cutting a fried flounder,
packed roe staring through a cough of steam—

I couldn't see their eyes, only
the mass of them. I could only feel

the cold wind tousle my hair,
          passing rudely through that
                    studded
                              field

a year and then another year (taegeuki)

samara tassel the crowded maples—
a strong wind winnows each overripe kiss.
none in their fast dance expect not to root.

a cold rain tears down the curtain of ash.
the city, naked wet and ungendered
exhales the gray petrichor of asphalt.

a wet road clothed with mulching leaves, moonlight,
the stormdrain chugs the world through iron teeth:
remnants of autumn milled by through traffic.

incense smoke unspooled by no one, nothing.
my voice is pulled wide by the empty room.
even your absence is mocked by my breath.

Walking Shadow

The yellow lily laughs
at its own joke. Someone has to break.

Spring means beauty and chaos and
beauty means chaos and chaos

is a whale's breach: fun and pumice; itch
slapped with body and world

Drafting my goodbyes

the sun punches through rain, stains
each impossible drop like glass;

your laughter and your touch
heavy on my soaked clothes. I know

you'll want to die again soon.
the sun is nothing new.

Nibble Fish

In some dreams I find her sober—
a tongue cut on rock candy.

She says each night took its own small bites,
a slow feast of her decay.

It must be those dreams that wake you up
with sleep-talk apologies.

Colorado River, etc.

I hate a graveyard's clogged pores, the sweat
of a California sprinkler—

I hate the holiness
that gentrifies a corpse. Somehow

a fig begets its sugared wasps, wasps
melt into their sacred jam,[3]

3 The advent of the fig wasp brings life for both fig and wasp; as she sows her eggs around the syconium, she pollinates its flowers and spurs their growth into fruit. She dies and the swelling fig swallows her whole, body and blood. Her sons wake first to impregnate their sisters, dig escape tunnels, and die. Her daughters hatch pregnant, floured in pollen, to leave, find a new fig, and die. And so on and so on, nothing wasted.

Waste

The Suicide Prevention Lifeline
plays the funniest hold music.[4]

Sometimes irony suddenly dies,
my metaphors crumpled

in my pocket with receipts. Tonight
War starts. I have no choice but to sleep.

---

4 Melrose Moonlighters, Gary Stockdale

Inheritance is everything you don't deserve.

am I more than uncut ddeok?
"It takes just as long to grow one grain

as the whole pot," he says.
Infants take their first shits

having eaten nothing. It's so hard
to justify my life.

American Palimpsest

A price tag stripped off a box
leaves remnants like a day moon;

as stars poke holes through night's eyelid
pinprick guilt decorates your image.

Even flies rub reverent hands
before giving birth in a corpse

Portland Drum[5]

The timbre of a beaten crowd—
lungs pulled taut across brief phrases—

each night slaps with the same hand,
each day belts the same two verses:

some pledge allegiance to a burnt flag,
some to the stick that holds it.

5 Summer 2020

generic city poem, Korea, prior

Garlic pressed through a tight lattice—
buildings rose from a split clove

and beneath another cold scan
from another bloodshot sun, they

pulled shadows up like loose pants, let go
as knucklebone hills punched it closed.

I Don't Hate Japan

a king had silver chopsticks
so we all use stainless steel;

mine don't leave the small napkin
until my father takes a bite.

I pull pin-bones from a mackerel
but still find some in my teeth.

Baleen

the tongue scrapes pages for meat,
the prophet brines in the throat.

spite fills a ranula,
curtained by a smile-shaped rage—

rage that strains a mouthful of days
and keeps only what feeds it.

Parthenogenesis[6]

I was Sisyphus's kidney stone
I was my father's father's father

I am a mute love's metastasis
I am Sisyphus's kidney stone

my father tries to be his father:
to make me better, in his own way

---

6 Aphids are born pregnant. And the aphid inside that aphid: pregnant. And the aphid inside that aphid: pregnant. And all of them identical.

No Face[7]

it's a shape of fate: children starved
by a starved womb stack fat like bricks;[8]

"everything [he] never had"
popcorning from cupped hands—I tried

to chew his gold. Forgive me also
when I sluice you with my cravings:

---

7 Hayao Miyazaki based No Face's design off *Bombyx mori*, the domestic silkworm.

8 Numerous studies of adults exposed to starvation in gestation have demonstrated a significant association between prenatal exposure to famine and higher rates of obesity later in life (alongside related chronic illnesses). This is thought to be an epigenetic response to scarcity with effects that are not only permanent, but also, to some extent, inherited across multiple generations, although with adverse effects when children of famine grow up in their own plenty (Schulz, L. C. "The Dutch Hunger Winter and the Developmental Origins of Health and Disease." *Proceedings of the National Academy of Sciences*, vol. 107, no. 39, 2010.).
We learn our mothers' hungers while in the womb, just as we inherit our fathers' stress while still in the testicle (Seong, KH., Ly, N.H., Katou, Y. *et al.* Paternal restraint stress affects offspring metabolism via ATF-2 dependent mechanisms in Drosophila melanogaster germ cells. *Commun Biol* 3, 208 (2020).

繭

(Korean Declaration of Independence)

We hereby declare that Korea is an independent state and that Koreans are a self-governing people. We proclaim it to the nations of the world in affirmation of the principle of the equality of all nations, and we proclaim it to our posterity, preserving in perpetuity the right of national survival. We make this declaration on the strength of five thousand years of history as an expression of the devotion and loyalty of twenty million people. We claim independence in the interest of the eternal and free development of our people and in accordance with the great movement for world reform based upon the awakening conscience of mankind. This is the clear command of heaven, the course of our times, and a legitimate manifestation of the right of all nations to coexist and live in harmony. Nothing in the world can suppress or block it.

For the first time in several thousand years, we have suffered the agony of alien suppression for a decade, becoming a victim of the policies of aggression and coercion, which are relics from a bygone era. How long have we been deprived of our right to exist? How long has our spiritual development been hampered? How long have the opportunities to contribute our creative vitality to the development of world culture been denied us?

Alas! In order to rectify past grievances, free ourselves from present hardships, eliminate future threats, stimulate and enhance the weakened conscience of our people, eradicate the shame that befell our nation, ensure proper development of human dignity, avoid leaving humiliating legacies to our children, and usher in lasting and complete happiness for our posterity, the most urgent task is to firmly establish national independence. Today when human nature and conscience are placing the forces of justice and humanity on our side, if every one of our twenty million people arms himself for battle, whom could we not defeat and what could we not accomplish?

We do not intend to accuse Japan of infidelity for its violation of various solemn treaty obligations since the Treaty of Amity of 1876. Japan's scholars and officials, indulging in a conqueror's exuberance, have denigrated the accomplishments of our ancestors and treated our civilized people like barbarians. Despite their disregard for the ancient origins of our society and the brilliant spirit of our people, we shall not blame Japan; we must first blame ourselves before finding fault with others. Because of the urgent need for remedies for the problems of today, we cannot afford the time for recriminations over past wrongs.

Our task today is to build up our own strength, not to destroy others. We must chart a new course for ourselves in accord with the solemn dictates of conscience, not malign and reject others for reasons of past enmity or momentary passions. In order to restore natural and just conditions, we must remedy the unnatural and unjust conditions brought about by the leaders of Japan, who are chained to old ideas and old forces and victimized by their obsession with glory.

From the outset the union of the two countries did not emanate from the wishes of the people, and its outcome has been oppressive coercion, discriminatory injustice, and fabrication of statistical data, thereby deepening the eternally irreconcilable chasm of ill will between the two nations. To correct past mistakes and open a new phase of friendship based upon genuine understanding and sympathy — is this not the easiest way to avoid disaster and invite blessing? The enslavement of twenty million resentful people by force does not contribute to lasting peace in the East. It deepens the fear and suspicion of Japan by the four hundred million Chinese who constitute the main axis for stability in the East, and it will lead to the tragic downfall of all nations in our region. Independence for Korea today shall not only enable Koreans to lead a normal, prosperous life, as is their due; it will also guide Japan to leave its evil path and perform its great task of supporting the cause of the East, liberating China from a gnawing uneasiness and fear and helping the cause of world peace and happiness for mankind, which depends greatly on peace in the East. How can this be considered a trivial issue of mere sentiment?

Behold! A new world is before our eyes. The days of force are gone, and the days of morality are here. The spirit of humanity, nurtured throughout the past century, has begun casting its rays of new civilization upon human history. A new spring has arrived prompting the myriad forms of life to come to life again. The past was a time of freezing ice and snow, stifling the breath of life; the present is a time of mild breezes and warm sunshine, reinvigorating the spirit. Facing the return of the universal cycle, we set forth on the changing tide of the world. Nothing can make us hesitate or fear.

We shall safeguard our inherent right to freedom and enjoy a life of prosperity; we shall also make use of our creativity, enabling our national essence to blossom in the vernal warmth. We have arisen now. Conscience is on our side, and truth guides our way. All of us, men and women, young and old, have firmly left behind the old nest of darkness and gloom and head for joyful resurrection together with the myriad living things. The spirits of thousands of generations of our ancestors protect us; the rising tide of world consciousness shall assist us. Once started, we shall surely succeed. With this hope we march forward.

Three Open Pledges

1. Our action today represents the demand of our people for justice, humanity, survival, and dignity. It manifests our spirit of freedom and should not engender antiforeign feelings.

2. To the last one of us and to the last moment possible, we shall unhesitatingly publicize the views of our people, as is our right.

3. All our actions should scrupulously uphold public order, and our demands and our attitudes must be honorable and upright.

The First Day of March of the 4252nd Year (1919) of the Kingdom of Korea

Son Pyong-hui, Kil Son-ju, Yi Pil-chu, Paek Yong-song, Kim Wan-gyu, Kim Pyong-jo, Kim Chang-jun, Kwon Tong-jin, Kwon Pyong-dok, Na Yong-hwan, Na In-hyop, Yang Chon-baek, Yang Han-muk, Yu Yo-dae, Yi Kap-song, Yi Myong-yong, Yi Sung-hun, Yi Chong-hun, Yi Chong-il, Lim Ye-hwan, Pak Chun-sung, Pak Hui-do, **Pak Tong-wan**, Shin Hong-shik, Shin Sok-ku, O Se-chang, O Hwa-yong, Chong Ch'un-su, Choe Song-mo, Choe Rin, Han Yong-un, Hong Pyong-gi, and Hong Ki-jo

Rumspringa

Mussels bound to black rock
send larvae out to drift.

When they tie their own beards to stone
will they lament the ocean's pull—

how the tide chokes rocks with life
dragged up and down by the same moon?

I only know these stories as they were given to me.

I stem from a line of rebels. My father's mother's father's father signed that paper knowing he'd be arrested. I don't know if he had prepared for torture. I don't know if he expected exile—if he knew that he'd die on an island without ever coming back to see the nation he asserted. I don't know if it was selfish. When they stoked those words across the peninsula they must have understood what would happen. Japan killed more than 7500 people in that movement, injured more than 16,000, arrested three times that. Arrests often meant torture, sometimes execution without trial. Japan tortured organizers to death, executed them publicly. Japan fired into the non-violent crowds. Japan herded the villagers of Jeamri into a church and shot them through the walls, then torched the building and the bodies. And so on and so on. If he had known, if he had been shown the bodies beforehand would he have signed it? What image would have stopped him? Any of them? Whose body? There are two kinds of anger. Anger with direction drives action, spurs purpose, claws at change. It is the inflammation of the wound, the pitched and focused scream of a kettle. Nameless rage—anger without outlets—is only pain. To have direction paired with powerlessness is a gun with a blocked barrel. Sound and fury. Korean people have so much of both. I know that his son resented him. He grew up to become an English professor and an asshole, gave up on his daughters when their mother died, came back to live with them decades later in the States, penniless and fluent. He flushed his cigarette butts, smoked his pipe alone, wrote nothing and burned things quietly until he died. My grandmother, in her youth, loved to write poetry. I think there is such a thing as an objectless grief. The wickless burning of a star. I think there is such a thing as inheritance.

Contract

a name binds two bones by the joint
and tugs in its own direction

his tensed beneath my skin,
hard from constant pulling—

and how many others move me now,
trace my parts with valley and shadow?

Knowing the Fish Pavilion[9]

Icarus fin unzips sky
stripping the algaed pond.

From above, these rorschach koi
are clothed with slothing lilies.

Does the fish who sips the summer's dross
feel the sun prefer its inkblots?

---

9 239 Northwest Everett Street, Portland, OR

DMZ Fable

Bear defuses her last garlic. God
splays her with the cheek of his knife,

peels her by the snout, plucks her claws,
sculpts a woman out of hunger, permits

the last Korean tiger
pawing at a land mine.

Waste

The young write to be heard, to be
understood. Death twirls its cattle prod.

Poems of the old are a face
smashed into plaster. A substitute

for children. Ego's autotomy.
Blood from the horned lizard's eye.

the Smell inside my own walls

the moon on its winking arc,
the sun on its cosine

punctuate time in turn
like the eyes of a scallop—

so many windows to one muscle,
pumping itself through an unfelt Brine

Cyclothymia

this full moon is a hole in the sky—
a manhole, cover scraped aside,

leaking honey, milk, propping open
salted eyes. I want to climb out,

to ask God if He seasoned Manna
with anything other than Hunger.

Cyclothymia

this Moon is a hole in the sky—
the far mouth of a tomb.

I want to climb out and look for you
beyond this granite dusk,

but for now I'll drink the dripping light
before the coming nights drag it closed.

Cyclothymia

This moon is an ebbing grin.
Sisyphus trips on the way down.

Walking like a broken bird
through touch and interchangeable touch . . .

Years laminate each tree.
These dry nights furrow the grain.

Again, That Briefest Season

Stellata beaks explode
into wallets of white tongues

toasting themselves like coconut,
hungover like they know

how long they still have to lap sweet breeze,
french-kiss affectionless beetles[10]

10 The magnolia family is thought to be among the most ancient and primitive flowering plants. Predating bees and butterflies, magnolia flowers evolved to depend on beetle pollination. Beetles, however, are inconsiderate, gorging indiscriminately with mouthparts that know only how to chew. Millions of rude springs have leathered magnolia tepals and calloused reproductive parts into hard cones. While most plants and their pollinators coevolved sophisticated symbioses, the oldest among them makes only accommodations, excuses.

Salganea Taiwanensis[11]

I want to know if it hurts, to let
kisses icepick hypotheticals;

I want to know if it hurts less
when you give yourself to the mouth, less

when your own mulls that smell of mulch
with a bubble-soap wing's umami

11 Taiwanese giant wood roaches mate for life, and unlike the prodigal romance of mantids, they practice a pragmatic, mutual cannibalism; once they find their partners and their rotting log and decide to share it, they take consensual turns nibbling each other's wings away. They no longer need them. Everything they could want—their lives together, their children, their banquet of decay—already stuffing their home's veins, the option of freedom is only encumbering.

Though my broken nose affords no fragrance

persimmons on a leafless tree
hang like notes from hammered strings.

Winter koi suspended:
beads of warm fat in broth

greasing the reflection
of a cold and tasteless sky.

Beau Geste[12]

The moon can't afford color; black mass:
huddled trees share their silhouettes—

2 coyotes sing 8 parts; lightless
woods stuffed with folk cadenza.

My window shut. Their high notes pop, fade
like bullets sown in ocean

---

12 The Beau Geste hypothesis, coined by the Right Honourable Lord John Krebs (the son of the Krebs cycle Krebs) in 1977, suggests that many animals wield wide and elaborate vocalization repertoires as a mechanism for defending territory through the illusion of population density. The hypothesis is named after the 1924 book, Beau Geste, wherein outnumbered soldiers prop up dead bodies to give the illusion of having more men. Coyotes, in attempts to establish territory or drive off perceived threats therein, sing while alternating rapidly between howls, barks, and yips of different speeds and pitches. Manipulating their variety of sound in tandem with how that sound travels through their environments, two coyotes can create the auditory illusion of seven or eight. These group songs are produced primarily by mated pairs and their children to claim their homes, we assume, but that might be projection.

this Side of Exile

from where you stand, can you also feel   toes chew bonemeal sand, bits of shell
the tallow of this heavy sun   minced by wave, interchangeable wave

if I trace my shoreline far enough
this Water takes a different name

Pillar of Salt

when will it go unpunished, looking
back? Where is that wrathless town?

Saigon, Seoul, that northern village, rolled
like clay between earth and brimstone sky—

my grandmother's afraid to cook.
She still thinks you'll hate the smell.

Horse and Sparrow

and that was our Babel:
the outhouse stalagmite.

and then a yard. a locked door.
lamplight pissing through windows.

This Fall the trees all torched together;
one night's wind licked them clean.

Foundations of a Great Wall

The loom chews boiled wormspit
to weave an emperor's clothes—

uncounted little bodies
bob naked in the wake.

Fear spins sinew into voiceless stone,
leaves the mute bones we tread.

That Shitty Apartment

spent incense collapses
into candy cigarette chunks

and spiced smoke diffuses
through a dimming conversation—

that evening's sweet vapors curtain
our kitchen's entropy.

Crockpot Requiem

I learned it from my father: the prod,
the third offer, a deaf outpouring,

"Have you had enough to eat?"
—tongue limping after hands—

raking lies with a slotted spoon,
the apology, even[13]

---

13 what I'm trying to say is

while we're both here
the moon's black in remission
the wicks of my fingers burnt to the first joint steam
still crouching under rice

I want to push apart jaws

of dusk and crepuscular
dawn fall through night's maw
deep gullet
with you for you

I want to be steam in the gut

a gizzard stone the ghost
of heat that coats your mouth
your throat your
chest your brain

I want to be swallowed whole

I want to be swallowed in parts each
called like disciples to a fork
my fibers braised in salt acid heat the gentle blood
of carrot-leeched sweetness

I want to be so tender and easily pierced

I want to fall apart
with you
for you
on you
I want to be September to a bear

I want to let you steal
desperately
naturally
from me

and be so honest in your leaving

if Adam and Eve weren't made hungry:

toy poodles being walked
past polnareffed hedges

in strollers. Good and Evil
fermenting on the bent branch.

no Word for shame. our unnamed bareness
a stakeless Imperfection.

Inheritance is everything you don't decide.

The birthmark on the tip
of my tongue looks like a scar.

Am I more than a plucked string
shaking off sound like a washed dog?

The scar on the tip of my tongue
I carved with my own teeth.

Rainier

Old, tepid volcano:
a sharp loose tooth chewing soft clouds.

As the drunk sun collapses
trees blend into matte silhouette.

The hawk riding currents I cannot feel
only ever looks down.

Saint Helens

mushrooms trumpet off a mulching log,
flies sow eggs in venison;

the mountain has powdered its crown—
young pines stubble an ashen slope.

See how it makes itself an alms bowl
molding over with snow?

絲

Sericulture

Is flesh palimpsest or translation?
Names collapse in the gut:

Bear is a lump of Summer;
Summer Spring's prodigal falling;

our souls—that colonnade of lotus—
still rooted in desire.

I only know these stories as they were given to me.

I stem from a line of rebels. For a long time my family in the north worshiped Demons. For a long time we prayed only out of fear. The fear was older than the garden; older than the house; older, even, than the Tree we built around. I think it began as something else, something closer to trust—a kind of vicarious confidence. The Tree, too, was probably beautiful then. We must have had a reason to make our home around the Demon Tree, but whatever that was, the years had fermented it. My father's father watched his grandmother leave offerings, make sacrifices, yoked with fear. He hated it. He said the house was always loud. Demons demanded sacrifices. He said the tree was where they lived. A hollow in the trunk. Growing up he knew fear and rage in too many languages. Taking a shovel and bucket to the outhouse, my father's father came back and choked the Demon Tree with human shit. His grandmother beat him out of fear. He chose, for all of us, his own inheritance.

Event Horizon[14]

Petals elope with spring breeze;
eternity like coffinwood, mulch,

above and below brief dreams—the earth
freckles so much space. My hairs

might take turns jumping, or fall
all at once like ginkgo leaves

---

14 A theoretical boundary beyond which no events can affect any observer—in the case of a black hole, the perimeter wherein the escape velocity is greater than or equal to the speed of light, thus keeping light contained. Similarly, the notion of a cosmic event horizon suggests that, given the expansion of the universe, there exists a maximum comoving distance from which light emitted now can affect any future observer. An infinity exists that we can never see. Existence, the observable—these are exceptions, bubbles in a black ocean.

Cobweb by the Window of the Tea House:

loose skin of an old woman's triceps
weakly kiting Fall breeze.

With each new shock these leaves lose strength;
I sip to discern the bath

when they've been washed of all worth
and can no longer bless my cup.

Ecclesiastes Dog

Shepherd bored into ouroboros;
we snuck Prozac in cheese.

She needed a yard, sheep, drugs
to truffle-pig for the TSA.

I pulled her teeth from my sister's hand.
That howl spread like a yawn.

Waste

Flames lap trash from the can,
A man sips the fire.

If meaninglessness exists
then it, too, burns. How much of the moon

must I drink to siphon sunlight?
Share with me before the flood.

Nothing New

I'm always tired in spring—
newborn blossoms already balding.

"It's always a metaphor with you,"
she says, but I can't help it;

a sneeze of petals. I'm always
drafting my goodbyes.

A poem, like a life, is made
from dust. Skin our bodies tithe. Like lives

letters congregate to make
Meaning. Meaning

pollutes every dialogue. Dust
and dust in their furtive dance.

But a worm chewed through the vine[15]

rain baleens us by the doors,
the clouds a soft palate. You joke

they eat shirts out of spite. I say
a silk-moth has no mouth, only

smell, flapless wings, unspent
genitals. Probably this anger.[16]

---

15 Jonah 4:7

16 한(恨)

Conjugation of Lordless Body

My father made me be a man,
demanded his reflection.

I starved myself into a man,
foie gras-ed myself with protein.

A lover wants me as a man, bends
herself into a question.

This isn't what I'm supposed to say:

In an Octopus's Garden

Hope and I part amicably—
a band-aid, left alone

learns to trust. Damp skin gasping.
What persists: the body

I steward, a ledger
of inheritance, desire;

Noble Eightfold Desire:

desire who fruits on the nude branch,
desire in her aggressive orbit,

desire in the shape of a wound,
keloid desire in her own shape blooming,

limpet desire poxing black rock,
desire like tide like moon like collateral sand.

Desire the orphan mother scatters her young having saved

nothing. Taught nothing. Desire
begets desire. I am a man

when I'm asked to be. You
holding yourself with my arms. You

wanting me. And what is desire but a void?
and what is a void but a moist grain?

and what is hope but an elm's shade in winter?

A Dragonfly's[17] Intinction[18]

For all your newfound freedoms
why cling to lotus in the pond?

Could you break your sunbaked wings
to stuff the effigy of youth?

Water glazed with today's sky
will never take you back.

---

17 Dragonflies are born underwater and spend the majority of their lives as fully-aquatic nymphs, only crawling out into dry air at the epiphany of adulthood. Nymphs bear little resemblance to their fully-realized neon cruciform bodies; at this stage they lack their wings, color, and sexual organs, but do feature an extendable hydraulic jaw that they use to catch invertebrates, tadpoles, and small fish. The irony of a dragonfly's life is that, while adulthood grants it flight and near limitless freedom of movement, it can never reenter the water. Nostalgia becomes an asymptote. The only time a dragonfly will touch the surface again is a brief dip to deposit eggs she can't protect, watching the cycle repeat through her own reflection.

18 Intinction: the action of dipping the bread into the wine (or Welch's) at Eucharist. Not all denominations do it. Different feasts for different priests.

Buddha hears about cell theory and laughs, vindicated

A pang that wakes up before me,
threads our chests together—I think

it's penance for meiosis; I feel
you as a phantom limb.

Raindrops stranded on my window
kiss to rebuild the cloud.

Things That Don't Taste the Same Here

번데기

a silkworm spins expensive clothes and grows
into its own stiff cocoon

now useless except to be steamed
served in newspaper cones

baby teeth press beondegi
hot gush like summer mud in toes

짜장면

choral slurp from across the street
reverse waterfalls of jjajangmyeon

the aroma disrobes in warm wind
flashes hints of pork and dark sweetness

meat and maltose wink reminds the boy
of the insects in his own mouth

기대

he promised the smell he'd come back rich
treat his mother at the noodle house

but his young dreams have grown cold
after forty sojourn years

my father has found wealth in this country
but never jjajangmyeon that satisfied

The Didactic Breath

The anticyclone unspools
to clothe the cyclone. A cassette tape.

We stop hearing it, say the wind dies
down. Its dependents sag.

Flags drool in their naps. God
for a moment, forgets His loud point.

Proper Shading

Crying pines cross-hatch ripples
on a blue sky's reflection.

Stained loam moans petrichor; your splintered
trunk sighs such an honest smell—

prostrate elm broken twice: last night's breath
and again to clear the driveway.

Grateful Trespass

widowed avocado tree,[19]
you still pearl apostrophes.

Do you mind our small hands
pecking at your grief? I know

some ghosts who'd prefer to see
ants harvest their altar fruit.

---

19 Avocados are an example of evolutionary anachronism. Their flavor, texture, and size coevolved alongside now extinct American megafauna (giant ground sloths, gomphotheres, etc.), who would eat the trees' fruit and spread their seeds. They still cater to those giant ghosts, and without our hunger and hands would eventually join them in a peaceful obsoletion, their each fruit rotting near the trunk, season after season, attempt after attempt.

Gratitudes

삼짇날

the old man takes fresh steps
into the stillborn morning;

slow-sipped azalea wine:
gray light puddles on foreign streets.

He adds one to the cigarettes
littered like cherry blossoms

삼복

the young man breathes thick steam
pressing rich men's jackets.

Simmering like a plucked chicken
damp air sticks to his skin and lungs

"the very sweat that pearls on your arms
will be our wealth, magnae"

추석

"then there were fire orders.
We'd be sent to a burned-down house

harvest blackened clothes from ash,
take them back and clean them,

but the smell and stain of soot—
that stayed with us long after."

섣달그믐

the old woman skipped lunches,
folding meals into the dry earth.

Pacing the infant garden
the old man sowed his time.

My own father sprouts gray hairs now
waiting for me to grow

A Pine Ignores the Seasons

Lake water ripples like bedsheets—
leaves drift in fever dream

the old pine bows to its reflection—
lichen beard tickles green image.

Suddenly, ducks smash their heads
through the opaque wavering.

How we choose to connect the stars

Walking on Orion's bloodless legs
you hunt invented shapes;

Clutching the Dipper
you sip from a waning moon.

Sew your skeleton embroidery
with the silk of your own life

Star and Comet[20]

The sea star and the orphan arm throb
with ghosts. They keep what they need:

a language for body, self. Acid
unravels and forgives.

What they stitch: new, full animals—
almost the same animal.

---

20 While most sea stars require an intact central disk (along with its mouth and digestive capacities) in order to regenerate, some species, like those in the genus Linkia, can build themselves back with nothing more than a fasting arm. Each limb contains the desire for wholeness and the code to bloom into it, redeeming amputation or autotomy into a kind of cloning. Before that process is complete, these single, divorced arms are called comets.

Leftovers for Breakfast

Parrotfish unspool coral;
spray of grain; legion. The enjambment

Of love and grief betrays the line
Of a good breakfast.

Onions, already chopped, confetti
Fried rice. Joy hisses in hot fat.

Inheritance is Massimo Bottura's grandma's tortellini

I didn't eat. Halmeoni fed me.
And I ate. And it was good.

If I have not love, then debt is just
a moon dragged along by ego,

fear. Am I more than the beg
of a balloon string, sound riding thread?

OTHER TITLES FROM THE SONG CAVE:

1. *A Dark Dreambox of Another Kind* by **Alfred Starr Hamilton**
2. *My Enemies* by **Jane Gregory**
3. *Rude Woods* by **Nate Klug**
4. *Georges Braque and Others* by **Trevor Winkfield**
5. *The Living Method* by **Sara Nicholson**
6. *Splash State* by **Todd Colby**
7. *Essay Stanzas* by **Thomas Meyer**
8. *Illustrated Games of Patience* by **Ben Estes**
9. *Dark Green* by **Emily Hunt**
10. *Honest James* by **Christian Schlegel**
11. *M* by **Hannah Brooks-Motl**
12. *What the Lyric Is* by **Sara Nicholson**
13. *The Hermit* by **Lucy Ives**
14. *The Orchid Stories* by **Kenward Elmslie**
15. *Do Not Be a Gentleman When You Say Goodnight* by **Mitch Sisskind**
16. *HAIRDO* by **Rachel B. Glaser**
17. *Motor Maids across the Continent* by **Ron Padgett**
18. *Songs for Schizoid Siblings* by **Lionel Ziprin**
19. *Professionals of Hope: The Selected Writings of* **Subcomandante Marcos**
20. *Fort Not* by **Emily Skillings**
21. *Riddles, Etc.* by **Geoffrey Hilsabeck**
22. *CHARAS: The Improbable Dome Builders* by **Syeus Mottel** (Co-published with Pioneer Works)
23. *YEAH NO* by **Jane Gregory**
24. *Nioque of the Early-Spring* by **Francis Ponge**
25. *Smudgy and Lossy* by **John Myers**
26. *The Desert* by **Brandon Shimoda**
27. *Scardanelli* by **Friederike Mayröcker**
28. *The Alley of Fireflies and Other Stories* by **Raymond Roussel**
29. *CHANGES: Notes on Choreography* by **Merce Cunningham** (Co-published with the Merce Cunningham Trust)

30. *My Mother Laughs* by **Chantal Akerman**
31. *Earth* by **Hannah Brooks-Motl**
32. *Everything and Other Poems* by **Charles North**
33. *Paper Bells* by **Phan Nhiên Hạo**
34. *Photographs: Together & Alone* by **Karlheinz Weinberger**
35. *A Better Place Is Hard to Find* by **Aaron Fagan**
36. *Rough Song* by **Blanca Varela**
37. *In the Same Light: 200 Poems for Our Century From the Migrants & Exiles of the Tang Dynasty,* translated by **Wong May**
38. *On the Mesa: An Anthology of Bolinas Writing (50th Anniversary Edition),* edited by **Ben Estes and Joel Weishaus**
39. *Listen My Friend, This Is the Dream I Dreamed Last Night* by **Cody-Rose Clevidence**
40. *Poetries* by **Georges Schehadé**
41. *Wings in Time* by **Callie Garnett**
42. *Two Murals* by **Jesús Castillo**
43. *Punks: New & Selected Poems* by **John Keene**
44. *ABC Moonlight* by **Ben Estes**
45. *Star Lake* by **Arda Collins**
46. *The Maybe-Bird* by **Jennifer Elise Foerster**
47. *Seriously Well* by **Helge Torvund**
48. *Dereliction* by **Gabrielle Octavia Rucker**
49. *Bookworm: Conversations with* **Michael Silverblatt**
50. *April* by **Sara Nicholson**
51. *Valley of the Many-Colored Grasses* by **Ronald Johnson**
52. *The Sphinx and the Milky Way: Selections from the Notebooks of* **Charles Burchfield**
53. *Telling the Truth as It Comes Up: Selected Talks & Essays 1991–2018* by **Alice Notley**
54. *Lunar Solo: Selected Poems* by **Jules Laforgue**
55. *Stranger* by **Emily Hunt**
56. *The Selkie* by **Morgan Võ**
57. *Hereafter* by **Alan Felsenthal**
58. *Cold Dogs* by **Zan de Parry**
59. *Saturday* by **Margaret Ross**
60. *Many Poems* by **Roberta Iannamico**
61. *Ultraviolet of the Genuine* by **Hannah Brooks-Motl**